Rattlesnake Karma

Richard Sutphen

Rattlesnake Karma

Malibu, California

For a catalog of books
and over 300 self-help and
self-exploration tapes,
write:

Valley of the Sun
Box 38, Malibu, CA 90265

Cover Photo by Tara Sutphen, January 1985. Taken at the Casa Grande, Hohokam Indian ruins near Coolidge, Arizona. Built about 1350, this three-story structure of unreinforced adobe dominated the village in which it was built. Archeologist studies suggest that it was used for astronomical observations.

First Printing: June, 1985
Valley of the Sun Publishing
Box 38, Malibu, California 90265
Box 5800, Scottsdale, Arizona 85261

ISBN Number: 911842-39-X
Library of Congress Card Number: 85-050289

To my wife,
Tara

Our relationship
is a dream from
which I hope to
never awaken.

Other Books By The Author
Poetry
Sometimes The Words Of Love Have No Words - 1970
A Deep Breath Of Yesterday - 1970
I Love To Have You Touch Me - 1971
Burying Pompeii - 1972
Open Hand Love - 1974
Spirit Mountain Speak To Me - 1977

Also

The poetry book **Your Voice Makes My Knees Tickle** was written under the name Todd Roberts. Richard edited **The Sensitivity Tree,** which included his work and that of five other poets. He has authored eight non-fiction metaphysical books and three general market titles in addition to compiling 14 books for the professional art/advertising market. His publishers include, Simon & Schuster Pocket Books, McGraw-Hill Book Company, W. H. Allen (England), Art Direction Book Company, Sutphen Studio and Valley of the Sun Publishing.

Contents

Holy War

On The Road

Tara & Home

To me, writing poetry is the purest form of automatic writing. I've never been able to write a good poem about something because I wanted to write a good poem about something. I can't force the words. They just happen in response to experiences. So, I wait until the words of my life jump into my mind and then simply transfer them to paper.

My poetic goal is always to capture a moment, an emotion or a concept using a minimum of words with maximum impact. And impact is simply your personal reaction to the words. What does the poem create within you? Hopefully, somewhere between the covers of this volume are pages that will make you smile, or force you to remember, or touch a fantasy, or make you mad, or cause you to switch religions. The bottom line is, did you identify?

This is my seventh poetry book and the first since 1977. The early volumes received wide distribution through Crown Publishing. After the release of **Spirt Mountain Speak To Me** in 1977, I wrote little poetry for six years. I don't know if I wasn't inspired or was just too busy. It was a frantic period in which I wrote several non-fiction books, and encompassed a move from Arizona to Malibu, California, in 1979. Today, because I can't decide which I like best, I maintain residences in both California and Arizona.

Since you already have the book in your hands, it is probably too late to inform you that it contains language and opinions that are sure to be objectionable to quite a few people.

Transitions

CAN'T HIDE

I can't hide
    from myself
    in a poem

Emotions emerge
    and write
    themselves

    as I observe

    not knowing
    whether to
    laugh or cry.

ANSWERING MACHINE

I sit alone watching
    the sun set
    into the Pacific

A sea breeze fills
    the room with
    cool salt air

The fireplace tosses
    dancing reflections
    onto the glass

And gentle lute music
    provides
    the background —

    the phone rings,
    but I only answer
    in my mind:

"Hello, this is a recording.
I'm not here now.
I'm back in 1970 walking
on a Mexican beach.
If you'll leave your number
I'll call you when I return."

Malibu, California
December 1982

JETÉ

She dances alone
on a crystal bridge
suspended between
reality and illusion

        on one toe
        then the other
        turning
        turning
        oblivious
        smiling
        on one toe
        then the other

        descending

        slowly

        into madness.

ANOTHER DELUGE

It's been raining
40 days and nights
and I'm building another
ark to save my world

Working in the rain

Pretending to care

Building an ark
        that
        won't
        float.

RATIONALES

We're all so good
 at manipulating
 circumstances
 to justify
 what we want
 to happen

And all because
 we're too
 chicken-shit
 to do what
 we really
 want to do
 without
 an excuse.

TOO SHORT

The message emerged
from the cosmos
in huge red letters
against my
fading reality

"Life is too short
 to dread weekends!"

It made me feel better.

IN THE DIRECTION OF CHANGE

The alienation
builds slowly

surely

until change
is assured

and you start
the process
all over again.

IN SHEEP'S CLOTHING

Why are you so
unwilling to
acknowledge the
creative potential
of your own
destructiveness?

TONGUE SCRAPER

We lived together
through two or
three months of
joint transition

She was a vegetarian
zealot who was
learning to live on air

And I awoke each
morning to a tape of
East Indian chants

She used sacred
Sai Baba ashes in
everything she cooked

Consequently everything
we ate tasted
like Sai Baba

But she taught me
to use a tongue scraper

and today

each morning and night
as I watch the plaque
circle down the drain
I
think
of
her.

SOME ARE CERTIFIABLE

None of the people
I know who are
stark raving crazy

think they are crazy

        not
        one

and it bothers me
        because
        I don't
        think
        I'm
        crazy.

YELLOW BRICK ROAD

Instead of clinging
so tenaciously to
your misery
    why not
    walk the
    Yellow
    Brick
    Road?

Could the wicked
witch of the North
be any worse than
it already is?

SHE WANTED TO HIDE

You're ashamed and
you wish
you could hide

O.K. ...

Bring your right hand
up to your face
and grab your
lower lip tightly
very
tightly

Now ...

Pull it slowly and
steadily up over
the top of your
head ... and ...
down ...
the
back ...

Great ...

You got your wish!

BEACHTOWN DATE

The storm-driven surf
  reflected the
  full moon

As we walked the
  seawall
  into the wind.

We kissed hello
  on the edge
  of the world

With nowhere to go
      but
      down.

PRE-DAWN HIGHWAY

My memories haunt
some dusty corners
of the Phoenix Valley
and the beaches of
Mexico and Malibu

      Ghosts

rattling their chains
      and laughing

a half crazy laugh
that ripples through
the illusions and fades
into the ground fog
that stretches before me.

...OH, WOW

She fucks with
the enthusiasm
of a stewardess
passing out
      peanuts.

LOVING TWO PEOPLE
AT ONE TIME

Being in love
without being
in love with
someone else
is a luxury
you could not
understand
unless you've
been there.

PROJECTION

You say
you read
between
the lines

well . . .

since you're
still smiling
I think you
read wrong.

THE SEARCH GOES ON

She is searching
for someone
prestigious
      to
      BE
before the lines
on her face
converge at the
Tuba City art show.

Day to Day

RATTLESNAKE KARMA

A diamondback rattlesnake lay coiled and exercising his tail on the ground beside my car. His message was loud and clear: "You ain't getting into this car, motherfucker!" He was the only snake I ever had to kill, but he was many rattles old and I think he had a death wish.

Rattlesnake encounters are part of living in Arizona and California if you **live** in Arizona or California and not in one of the master planned environments developers are constructing to look like a suburb of Detroit.

Over the years I've had countless skirmishes. In Arizona on two occasions, rattlers have gone swimming in my pool — once with three of my kids — but the kids and the snake all survived unmarked by the experience. Most of my snake meetings have taken place while exploring the back country or during early morning desert runs.

Once I put a new back door on my house but neglected to put an insulation strip under the door. Late one evening while sitting barefooted at my drawing board, I looked down to see a 36-inch rattlesnake about six inches from my toes. I captured him with a T-square and wastebasket and carried him out into the desert — the Pima Indian Reservation a half block from my house. Before letting him go we had a telepathic talk.

"Look . . . I don't want any rattlesnake karma so I'm letting you go. I live back there. You live out here. We can coexist. Tell your friends and family, O.K.?"

From then on, my neighbors on both sides continued to have their share of snake problems. But it was the last time I've even seen a rattlesnake. Three years later, one crawled into my ground-floor Malibu, California, office on Pacific Coast Highway. But he came to visit on a rare day I wasn't there, and my business manager turned him in to the fire department.

RATTLESNAKE ADVENTURE

At **Thee Pitts** barbecue
they offer rattlesnake
as an appetizer and
tourists from Minnesota
ask where the snakes
                 are from

"Local," they say,
"plenty of 'em right
 here in Scottsdale."

And the tourists leave
the restaurant scanning
the ground and doing
a quick-step
            back
            to their
            car

When they get home to
St. Paul they'll
tell their friends
of this adventure.

I WAS LIVING IN CALIFORNIA

Like his father
before him
my father was
born, lived
and died in
Omaha, Nebraska

He read about
California once

The article said
rats climbed the
palm trees and
made nests in the
dried branches

When the city
trimmed the trees
the rats came
tumbling down

My father told
me he wouldn't
live in a place
where rats fell
        out
        of
        trees.

K/ DEBT

He stuck his karma
between her legs
and ended up with
      a lot
      of debts
      to pay.

STATE GOVERNMENT

To attain the bookstore
business license
required being
fingerprinted
at the Los Angeles
County Jail
for examination
by the F.B.I.

And I could have purchased
a license
to sell guns
for less money.

It's very important
to keep criminals
out of the
bookstore business.

Los Angeles, California

STATE GOVERNMENT AGAIN

Behind the cage
   of the woman
   who would not
   loan me her pen
   was a sign...

"Small minds
   talk about people-
   Average minds
   talk about events-
   Great minds
   talk about ideas."

That sign was the
   only thing that
   saved my day.

Los Angeles, California

**AND GOD SAID, "THIS WILL CAUSE
HIM TO GET HIS ACT TOGETHER."
BUT IT DIDN'T.**

I once had a father-in-law
with hemorrhoids
who came in drunk
early Sunday morning
and turned on the TV

Oral Roberts was preaching

Oral said, "Touch the TV
and be healed!"

So father took down
his pants and sat
bare-assed on the set

and his hemorrhoids
went
away

forever.

TRAINED DOG

They are a
reclusive
couple who live
in a remote area
and never answer
their phone

nice people who
like to be alone
with the cute
little dog
they taught to
give head.

CORPORATE CLIMBER

She would have
fucked herself
all the way
to the top

    but

the president
preferred boys.

UNFADED RELECTIONS

I've progressed
to the level
of self-defeating
    behavior

in an attempt
to accelerate
the backslide
into a childhood
    fantasy

that never grew
    up.

LEAKY

He told me that
before he became
a vegetarian
he had a
leaky asshole

That was fifteen
years ago
but to this day
everytime I see
him I think,

"He used to have
 a leaky asshole."

PREDICTABLE OUTCOME #7

He built a
beautiful
castle of sand

on the water's edge
                at
                low
                tide

and he wonders
why it's gone.

THE LADY WHO LIVES IN YESTERDAY

She dances with
a shadow
and talks
to a dream

unseen
in the
empty chair

And the room is
filled with
laughter
and love

repeating
over and over
in her mind

And reflected in
the smile
she smiles
for no one
here.

MORE THAN I EVER WANTED TO KNOW

He told me about
his wife
a big redhead
with a hawklike
nose and
bird legs

When they make it
she makes
chirping sounds
with her
teeth and tongue

He calls it
"musical fucking."

LIP-SERVICE DREAMS

He relates grand schemes
for fame and glory

lip-service dreams
he stopped chasing long
                              ago

              and failed
              to tell himself.

DAGWOOD AND BLONDIE

They make a great pair
of real-life cartoons
without color or
meaningful dialogue

living their one dimensional
life as if it won't
appear on the
comics pages tomorrow.

BIRD IN NEST

They placed
a little
stuffed bird
in the middle
of her
pussy hairs
and took a
Polaroid
picture
which he
carries in his wallet

He shows it
to people
and says,

"Here's a
picture of
my bird."

AUNT GLADYS

My aunt was an
interior designer
and one of the
founders of
Carmel, California

As a teenager I'd
sometimes spend
part of my
summers with her

One night in '53 we
went to a foreign film

It was bad and we
walked out after
fifteen minutes

But she gave me some
advice that has
served me through
countless bad movies,
mediocre concerts
and amusement park
                    rides . . .

"Richard, never, ever
  pay to be punished!"

DOESN'T THE WORLD REFLECT ME?

He wonders why
everyone else
isn't where he is

Next year he'll
be somewhere else
and just
as amazed that
the world hasn't
followed him.

LOST IN A CENTURY CITY
OFFICE COMPLEX
IN LEVIS AND A T-SHIRT

Thousands of three-piece
    suits parading stiffly
    through the interlocking
    levels of big business

    neatly trimmed short
              hair

    "professionals" all . . .

And they look at me with
    instant animosity
    because I don't have
    to play their game

    because I'm not part
    of their corporate
    war of the worlds

    because I don't have
    a house in Beverly Hills
    and a wife that
    shops on Rodeo Drive

I talked to the guy on
    the elevator that gave
    me the long dirty look,

    "You've got a tomato
              sauce
              stain
              on your
              necktie!"

ANOTHER RELATIONSHIP
GOING . . . GOING . . .

Aware of
their
terminal
condition
they search
the ruins
for clues
to survive

uncovering
patterns

restoring
memories

desperately
trying to
rebuild
Pompeii.

Holy War

Richard on stage in Los Angeles

THROWBACKS

If the powerful
spiritual
leaders
of today

Are a reflection
of yesterday

Moses must have
been one
hell of a
snake oil
salesman.

IT WILL LIGHT UP HER LIFE

She gropes her way
through the dark
       night
       of the
       soul

searching for reasons
for her suffering

searching for an esoteric
neon dildo to give her
       life

       meaning.

EXTRA SUPER STRENGTH PLEASE

They want
Excedrin
for the mind
to take away
the blame

They think
if they can
justify their
absurdities
the pain
will go away.

TO AVOID DROWNING

Two by two, they
    enter the ark
    with the destiny
    of the species
    upon their shoulders

Seeking salvation
    everywhere
    but where it is.

ARIZONA RECRUITER

She serves the
planet by using
her cosmic cunt
to convert
cowboys to
the cult.

IMPROVING INFERIOR PEOPLE

The true believers
gather in their
white robes
on the hillside
in the rain

alchemists
of the New Age

united in their quest

secure in their vision

chanting insipid
    incantations
    to convert
    base people
    into gold.

WAITING TO BE SAVED

They float aimlessly
    on
    life-
    preserving
    dreams

Adrift on an ocean
    without
    beaches

Beneath a sky
    without
    a sun

Waiting to be saved…
    waiting
    waitin
    waiti
    wait
    wai
    wa
    w
    .

FOR JESS STEARN

The guru gave him
a great volume
which explained
all the secrets
of the universe

"Are you going
  to read it?"
  I asked

He picked it up

flipped through
the pages
      and
      said,

"I've never
  wanted to know
  this much
  about anything!"

THE CAMERAS SCAN THE AUDIENCE

The cameras scan the
audience of a
Jimmy Swaggart crusade

The cameras scan the
audience of a
Rajneesh gathering

The cameras scan the
audience of a
political convention

The cameras scan the
audience of an
est event

AND THE FACES ARE ALL
                   THE
                   SAME

Wide-eyed true believers
looking for salvation
in something bigger and
better than themselves.

   "And blessed be
   those who are
   only hooked on
   sex, drugs or
   rock and roll"

For they are far ahead
of the game and will
hopefully inherit the earth.

BHAGWAN LEFT INDIA

Bhagwan left India
to come to America
and eat Oregon

but he
bit off
a little
more than
he could

chew.

TERRY SAYS . . .

She told me I am
the center of the
universe

I'm going to have to
think about that

It may mean more
responsibility than
I want right now.

AND THAT'S WHAT IS

She was overweight
  and ugly

A wild-eyed priestess
  of the light
  who eats dogma
  and demands
  that you
  accept her shit.

**AT THEIR FIRST MEETING SHE LOOKED
DEEPLY INTO HIS EYES AND SAID,
"WE'VE KNOWN EACH OTHER IN A PAST LIFE."**

The true believers

The esoteric children
of the
light

build rainbow bridges
to transcend levels
of
sanity

dancing
for
each other
in the
dim light
of
their own
desperation.

AN AVOID

The light dreamers
    eye your crotch
    while pretending
    to listen

An enlightened multitude
    escaping reality
    by jacking
      each
      other
      off
    and calling it
    the real thing.

MARRIED TO ONE AND
IN LOVE WITH ANOTHER

He scaled the
pinnacle of his
career and waits
on the peak
with a
palm-reading gypsy

hoping for
guidance that
will carry him
safely through
his vacillation
and into the arms
of young love.

ONE OF THE CHOSEN JOINS

They join the
holy faith to
find a new identity
and their humility
breeds arrogance

"All who are not
 of this faith
            are
            evil!
All who will not
listen will perish!"

And they plot to
take over the
world beginning
with Oregon
or Louisiana
or if they're just
getting started
            maybe

Spider's Breath, Montana.

STALKING

The Manx kitten
   emits excited
   high-pitched sounds
   as he stalks a fly
   beneath the TV
   while a kinetic
   preacher
   begs for money.

Malibu, CA

JIMMY, JERRY, JAMES AND THE BOYS

Those who were once
the prey of snake oil
salesmen now have a
voice they support with
the checkbook symbols
of their faith

They sit shaking in
front of their screens
intimidated by a
changing world and
secure only in
yesterday's values

Accepting the venomous
salvation of the
flickering illusion
of a holy messenger

"Silence the Humanists!"

"Defeat the liberals!"

"Commit the homosexuals!"

"Stop the abortionists!"

"Burn the occultists!"

"Convert the Jews!"

"Merge the church and state!"

"Bring on the Inquisition!"

"And send in your dollars
  to keep the voice of God
                    on
                    the
                    air!"

THE DARK AGES RETURN
ON CHANNEL 23 AT 8:30 A.M.

The Dark Ages could
be as close as the
millions of simple-
minded people who
support the televangelists
on the screen at
the foot of your bed.

PREVIEWS OF COMING RESTRICTIONS

The problem is

those who tithe
to the born-again
religious right
won't mind the
police state
they are
helping to create.

FORCEFULLY REMOVED

Werner Erhard's **est**
organization says that
most of those who don't
finish the **est** seminar
own their own business

That's because those
who own their own
business learn quickly
that to tolerate bullshit
does not lead to profit

> or
> enlightenment

> When I took
> away their
> microphone
> they called
> the police.

TO ALL THE PIOUS PREACHERS AND METAPHYSICALLY DISABLED

Enough of the sanctimonious
                              shit!

Spirituality isn't about
airy-fairy concepts, or white
light, or white robes, or
"talk" of love, or stopping
abortion, or repressing
homosexuals, or eliminating
secular humanism*. . .

Spirituality is about
accepting others
about
giving up judgment
about
detaching from negativity
about
accepting "what is"
about
giving up blame
about
serving the planet

The ultimate personal goal
of spirituality is probably
to go through a lifetime
with total involvement and
no disharmonious attachment
                              whatsoever.

---

*A term invented by the radical religious right to mean whatever
they want it to mean at the moment.

PURE ZEN

Study religion
and it will lead
to metaphysics
which will lead
            to
         Zen

Study them long
enough and deep
enough and you'll
come out the
other side and
realize the secret
is there is no
            secret

There is nothing
to seek and
nothing to find
and nothing
matters because
everything is
as it should be

You don't need
answers to find
            peace

The secret to
enlightenment is
when you are
hungry, eat;
when you are
tired, sleep;
when you are
horny, fuck.

On The Road

AFTER READING MY METAPHYSICAL BOOKS
THEY READ MY POETRY BOOKS

They invent me
because they need
to fulfill their
image of what
I must be to
do what I do

and

they resent me
when I let them
down by not
living up to
something
I never was.

COWBOY GLORY

I grew up on rodeos
and country music shows
that shaped my life
                    to
                    be

images of cowboy glory

boots and spotlights

applause and the next
                    town

... and "a shot of
Jack Daniel's straight up
and a cup of black
coffee to go with it!"

IT'S ONLY ROCK AND ROLL

Chasing an abstract dream
   through jet lag
   into places
   we don't belong

We've been on the road
   for twenty four cities
   that look just like
        the
        one
        before

Airports / limos / hotels
   $7000 out of pocket
   in tips alone . . .

"It's only rock and roll"
   and the reincarnation
   of a long-dead cowboy
        who
        should
        have
        known
        better.

BEFORE THE TALK SHOW

"I've heard a lot about you,"
    she said

"I don't know how to respond
        to that,"
    I said

"You don't look like I expected
        you to look,"
    she said

"How did you expect me to look?"
    I asked

"Like a spiritual person,"
    she said

"What do I look like?"
    I asked

"A cowboy!"
    she said

"I'm an Arizona spiritual
        person,"
    I said

"Oh," she said.

INFLUENCES

"Who were the people
that most influenced
you?" she asked

"Hank Williams and
his music ...
but he died!"

"James Dean and
his attitude ...
but he died!"

"Carson McCullers
and her novels ...
but she died!"

"Richard Brautigan
and his poems ...
but he died!"

"Jane Roberts
and her concepts ...
but she died!"

"Sam Shepard
and his words ...
Sorry,
Sam!"

I-10, AZ/CA BORDER

Lost in the middle
    of a maze

       with every path
       leading back
       to the border

Crossing the line
    only to find
    it before me

Watching for signs
    that don't appear
    on highways
    that don't exist

Chasing an illusion
    as if
    it mattered.

LOW BATTERIES

Acknowledge the applause
    act alive
    be friendly
    act humble
    be si . . .
    be si . . .
    be si . . .

    (switch circuits)

Acknowledge the applause
    act alive
    be friendly
    act humble
    be sincere.

TRAPPED

Prying questions
unrequested opinions
meaningless stories
undesired adulation
idle chatter and
small talk
      talk
      talk

and I retreat
      retreat
      retreat
      deeper
      into myself . . .

identifying with
the Indians' belief
in the obscenity
of the white man's
need to verbalize
      everything

      and detesting
      his intense
      fear of silence.

I DON'T WANT TO KNOW

Don't tell me
your stories of
your pain and
your glories

Their value is
in your knowing
not in mine

Tell them to
someone who
will pretend to
be interested

So in return you
will listen to
them and pretend
to be interested.

Or to a Ph.D.
who will pretend
to be interested
for $75 an hour

Or to a priest
who will pretend
to be interested
to get to heaven.

SPREAD YOUR CHEEKS, JIMMY

In a remote motel room
   on a TV with one
   channel I watch
   a televangelist
   denounce Darwin
       homosexuals
       and
       astrologers

And I'm sitting here
   smiling at my fantasy
   of the preacher being
   porked by a gay
       astrologer
       who doesn't
       believe in
       Adam and Eve.

SHATTERING THE BARRIER

Carried by forces
I can't see and
don't understand
to the far side
of a subjective veil

Where she stands
    silhouetted
    in the mist

  "Who are you?"
  I ask

"Your inspiration!
 Your revenge!
 Your executioner!"
   she laughs
   and laughs

   a mad
   metallic
   laugh
   that echos
   across the
   universe

   and back again

   shattering
   the barrier
   between
   her world
   and mine.

LEGENDS

The first legend wore
    his worn-out cloak
    of objectivity
    backwards to
    hide his hard-on

The second legend wore
    her oversized
    Ph.D.s to hide
    the fact
    she wasn't there

The third legend wore
    his insanity
    openly for he
    was far too far
    gone to hide

"Behind every legend
    is another story."
    said my famous
    friend, from beneath
    his barstool.

Malibu, California
Baja Cantina

ON THE ROAD AGAIN

Stuck in a hotel lobby
waiting for a late limo

I'm approached by a
white-robed purist

"Some of your concepts
 aren't spiritual!"
 he says firmly

"O.K.," I say

"What do you mean O.K.?"
                he asks

"I mean I'm not interested
 in what you think," I say

"Who do you think you are?"
                he asks,
                indignantly

I smile and quietly, like
Buddah, say…"The motherfucker
who is going to drop kick
your ass down those stairs."

He leaves immediately
                secure
in the accuracy of
his initial assumption.

SOMEWHERE BETWEEN

Is it for the
          glory

Or do I really
          care?

Answers get lost
     between the
     applause and
     the addictions

"It's still a
     rip off,"
     you said . . .
     "and it sure
     beats 9 to 5."

     "I agree!"

And somewhere
     between the
     research and
     the stage
     I slipped off
     the cutting edge
     of consciousness

     landing on
     the punch line
     of a joke
     that was stale
     in 1977.

Inspired by
B.J. Thomas on
his tour bus
somewhere between
Sedona and
Second Mesa:
January 1985

UP YOUR EARTH BURGER

Don't ask for a
shot of Jack Daniels
in a fancy
vegetarian restaurant

It makes the waiter
                    mad

He wants you to
drink a wine and
apple juice swizzle

"I'll settle for
 Jim Beam," I said

                but he
                didn't
                smile.

BODHISATTVA

The silence is broken
by the s-s-swish
of a Samurai sword

 severing illusion

and it rolls across
the floor leaving
a bloody trail of

truth.

TOO MANY ONE TWO MANYS

Too many
one
too manys

too many airports
       and
       hotels

too many expectations

too many simple-minded
       people looking
       for someone
       to follow

too many commitments
       and
       too many
       bills

       too many
       too little
       and
       too much.

BUT I'LL DO IT ANYWAY

Seduced by dreams
I never dreamed

Possessed by potentials
that could be . . .

A Silver Eagle waits
in the shadows
and an electronic
tube flickers
in my head.

I don't want to look
back
at what could have
been

although I know it
doesn't matter

It never did and
it
never
will.

Tara & Home

Tara Sutphen

DESTINY

The concept of
destiny is
the only real
mystery in life.

By comparison,
all others
are simply
books that sit
unread upon
a dusty shelf.

MEETING MY WIFE

I threw the party to
announce the video
and my house was
filled with movie stars
      writers
      producers
      astrologers
      and
      psychics

but I saw only you

and you saw only me

and I took your hand
      and
      you
      followed
      me
      down
      the
      stairs
      and
      into
      tomorrow.

Malibu, California
February 19, 1983

TARA

My first thought
    upon meeting
    you . . .

  "She's the
    most beautiful
    woman I've
    ever seen."

Jet-black hair,
    light-green eyes,
    fair complexion
    and a smile that
    melted my heart

You were dressed
    in skin tight
    black jeans
    and red
    cowboy boots

A Hollywood model
    who gave it up
    to be alone
    on a small ranch
    in Washington

You talked about
    your six-year-
    old son,
    your horses
    and cats

I was in love
    with you
    before I knew
    your last name.

Malibu, California
February 19, 1983

WE BOTH KNEW

As we made love
    the first time

I stopped and
    looked into
    your eyes —

"We both knew
    didn't we?"

You smiled and
    nodded,
    "Yes, we
    both knew . . ."

And you held me
    as if it would
    have to last
    for a lifetime.

Malibu, California
March 1983

ONLY A DREAM

Since our first
night together
we've held each
other in sleep
as if we fear
awakening to
find we were
only a dream.

Malibu, California

I ARGUE WITH YOU

Sometimes you tell me
    you are
    moody and impatient

    and I argue with you
    for you are
    the least moody and
    most patient lady
    I've ever known

Sometimes you tell me
    you look terrible
    when you are
    without makeup
    and your hair is
    tossed and tangled

    and I argue with you
    for you are
    always the most
    beautiful woman
    in the world to me

Several times a day
    you tell me
    that you love me

    and I never
    argue with you.

Malibu, California

HOT TUB

Do you think
the other
people in the
hotel hot tub
thought you
were just
sitting on
my lap
having a
conversation?

CONFLICT AND LOVE

You have my love —
    more than I
    knew I had

Sometimes I haven't
    shown it
    and you should
    have left

But you didn't

You understood
    my conflict
    and patiently
    waited until
    I recognized
    what you
    always knew

And you showed
    me more love
    than I knew
        you
        had.

I SEE YOU

I close my eyes
    and see you
    jogging beside me
    running graceful
    and free

I see you on
horseback
the perfectly
poised rider

I see you
laughing with
the children

talking to
your animals

drinking wine in
a Hawaiian sunset

sunbathing nude
on the deck in Malibu

playing Frisbee
on the beach

eating Italian food
in Greenwich Village

crying over the dog
we couldn't take home

beside me trailering
the horses south

beneath me in a
candlelit bedroom

I can't close my eyes
    and not see you.

Malibu, California

WEDDING DAY

You looked so beautiful
    in your simple
    white dress
    holding an armful
    of wildflowers

    the sea breeze
    tossing your
    long hair across
    your face as
    you said, "I will"

You leaned into me
    and smiled
    from across
    the barriers of
    lifetimes past

    the gulls laughed
    in the sky above
    and the surf
    pounded the
    sand below

Tomorrow is ours
    for the asking
    as was written
    very very
    long ago

"I love you my wife."

March 2, 1984
Malibu, California

CASA MARINA:
KEY WEST, FLORIDA

The ceiling fan spins
    hypnotic shadows
    around the room

    darting across the years

    over the hand-carved
    woodwork of craftsmen
    who have
    long since died

The hotel was built
    in the twenties

    flourished

    and then closed
    for thirty years

Today it lives again
    under a new tile roof
            new paint
            and varnish

But the old wall photos
    reflect past glories
    and yesterday's faces

    the ghosts who walk
    the refurbished hallways

    confused

    but no longer alone.

Honeymoon

HOYT AXTON'S MOTHER

Midnight, and we sit
    drinking beer in a
    funky open bar
    by the pier.

The folk singer
    offers to buy
    a drink for anyone
    who knows who
    wrote the song
    he's about to sing

You laugh and jab
    me in the ribs,
    knowing I usually
    know such trivia

"Hoyt Axton's mother,"
    I yell

I get a free beer

Afterwards he comes
    over to talk
    and for the first
    time I introduce
    you as my wife

God, it felt good.

Honeymoon

LATE AFTERNOON AT THE CASA MARINA

Through the fluttering
    curtains I catch
    glimpses of
    silhouetted sailboats
    as we make love

The sun is setting

We move in rhythm
    to familiar lyrics
    from a folk singer
    who entertains
    three floors below

Our favorite pastime

Only this time it's
                different . . .

You're my wife now
    and somehow that
    adds another dimension
    to the intense love
    I feel for you

"Did you 'come' better
    as a married woman?"

Honeymoon

I ALWAYS RETURN

The desert's call
   echos forever
   within my mind

I hear the spirits
   dance in the
   crevices between
   their world and
         mine

Chanting their songs
   for those
   who can hear

   "Join us!"

   "Join us!"

They laugh on the
   midnight

And I return
    I
   always
   return.

Scottsdale, Arizona

WELCOME HOME, TARA

"Welcome home,"
    I said

    We sat eating
    cowboy beans
    at Pinnacle Peak

    Listening to the
    country band

    Looking down on
    the lights of the
    Phoenix Valley

"Thanks for inviting me,"
    you responded
    smiling from
    ear to ear
    and snuggling
    into my arm.

Scottsdale, Arizona

ROCK SPRINGS

Rock Springs, Arizona
General Store
&
CAFE

The waitress wears
worn Levis and
a faraway look

It's 104° outside

Lumpy red plastic
booths line the
whitewashed walls

It's 102° inside

The smell of gravy
and pinto beans
fill the air

Waylon's on the jukebox

The cowboy at the
counter memorized
the menu in '63

I'm always at home here

You have to love and
understand Arizona
to be at home here.

BUNS

Every time
you wear those
lavender pants
that tuck
into your buns

I find a lot
of excuses to
walk behind you.

TIT PICTURE

While they all
watched
I drew a
funny face
on your
right tit

using your
nipple for
the nose

It was probably
the funniest
thing that
happened
this afternoon.

El Gulfo de Santa Clara,
Mexico - June 1984

ALMOST TO YUMA

You aim the 4-wheeler
    out of Mexico
    and into the
    desert night

Giving me a chance
    to find the
    words I lost
    in the sand

    Let's see ...
    here are
    a few ...

    sunburned
    recharged
    sex (lots of great)
    peaceful
    skinny dipping
    beach running
    shell searching
    fish eating

I'll put them together
            later.

RIGHT BACK

When I'm not
there for me
I can't be
there for you

But if you'll
only be patient

I'll be right back.

SPINNERS

Honey, look!
When we do
it this way
your tits spin
like two
    toy
    tops
trying to get
out of town
by sundown.

BEYOND THEIR FIELD OF VISION

You catch my eye
and eye my crotch
making suggestive
deep throat gestures

while I stand here
attempting to talk
seriously to people
I don't even know.

COMING

The semen
shot up
   up
   up
but it didn't
come down

Where the fuck
    did
    it
    go?

MALIBU NOVEMBER

The beach fades
into the fog ...

and

the grounded gulls
stand like statues
staring with
blind eyes into
their lost world.

CAT FOOD

Cat food
in a dish
on the patio

Mockingbird
eating the
cat food

Mockingbird
is cat food.

ARIZONA ADJUSTMENTS

The moving vans from
the midwest arrive
by the hundreds
bringing to Arizona
the simple-minded
middle-class that
always made the
middle of the country
a place to avoid

The only hope for
our state is balance

I propose a campaign to
bring in Californians

A Marin County gay
would stabilize five
Assembly of God
conservatives

A Malibu rocker
could convert at
least thirteen Future
Farmers of America

One good Hollywood
hooker would equalize
seven overweight
wives from Iowa.

TRAVIS - 7½

"Dad, in our next life
let's both come back
together as kids . . .

as brothers so we
can play together
all the time!"

"I'd really like that,
let's do it."

"Could we really?"

"I think so."

"Oh boy!"

TUMBLEWEED DAYS

The tumbleweed days
roll across the desert
and into the sunset
>> too fast
>> way
>> too fast

And I chase the days
> and you
> and the kids
> and the words
> and pictures
> and concepts
> across the desert
> and into the sunset
>> too fast
>> way
>> too fast.

Richard Sutphen is an author, poet, artist and seminar trainer who is best known for his metaphysical communications, including three Simon & Schuster Pocket Books titles: **You Were Born Again To Be Together, Unseen Influences** and **Past Lives, Future Loves.**

He has appeared on many TV shows such as **The Phil Donahue Show** and **Good Morning America.** In 1976, he conducted the first nationally broadcast past-life regression on **Tom Snyder's NBC Tomorrow Show.** A 1 3/4-hour **David Susskind Show** was built around Sutphen's work and is considered one of the series' most popular programs. In the last six years he has appeared on over 350 radio or television shows.

Sutphen has authored or compiled 33 books and over 200 self-help tape programs. He has a 17-year background in psychic investigation and human potential exploration. Over 40,000 people have attended his seminars which are conducted in approximately 24 cities each year.

Sutphen attended Art Center School in Southern California and originally worked as a highly awarded advertising agency art director. In the field of fine art he has had one man shows and taken top honors in major group shows.

Richard Sutphen

Poet Anthology 1970~1985

Publication: August, 1985~$5.95